THE Custom ART COLLECTION

Art for the
Eclectic Home

One-of-a-kind artwork *expertly* curated by

A Collection of Frameable, *Original Prints* from Top Artists

Ashley *and* **Jamin Mills**

The Handmade Home:
Creating a Haven for the Every Day

thehand
madehome
.net

Avon, Massachusetts

Published by
Adams Media, a division of F+W Media, Inc.
57 Littlefield Street, Avon, MA 02322. U.S.A.
www.adamsmedia.com

ISBN 10: 1-4405-7089-2
ISBN 13: 978-1-4405-7089-6

Printed in Mexico.

10 9 8 7 6 5 4 3 2 1

Cover images © Annie Bailey, Amy Tyler, Jan Skácelik, Yellena James, Ashley Mills, Ashley Percival.

This book is available at quantity discounts for bulk purchases.
For information, please call 1-800-289-0963.

Introduction

When you choose something for your home that you truly adore, it speaks to you. It moves you; it sparks something almost inexplicable in your soul. In the search for that gem, you create timeless spaces that tell the story of your life. By juxtaposing items that flow together in your own style, you become the ultimate composer of your spaces.

Now, with the forty inspiring pieces of art found within *The Custom Art Collection: Art for the Eclectic Home*, you'll be able to quickly and easily find that perfect addition to your space; that much-needed, one-of-a-kind creation! This carefully curated, eclectic array of inspiring pieces you'll find throughout are all from incredibly talented photographers, designers, and artists we love. With their participation and generosity, we are able to showcase a glimpse of their creations. Just for you!

Now that you've found pieces that you love, what next? The prints included here will fit any 8" × 10" frame, with limitless possibilities for matting and frame design. The perforated edge makes it easy to remove the images and create your own art gallery in just minutes!

When it comes to using art in your home, there are a lot of different opinions out there, and sometimes all those voices can be a little overwhelming. We believe, first and foremost, that you should do what feels right to you. But what do you do when in doubt? Here are three main categories we stick to when it comes to grouping art.

1. Color

- **Create Depth:** Use pieces that have varying shades in the same tones to create depth and interest on your walls. Consider this strategy with both frames and art. The frames are just as important, so let them work together to hold something beautiful on those walls.

- **Play with Contrast:** Think in terms of opposites and try to balance them. Bringing in an element like a metal frame and juxtaposing it with natural wood, or traditional art with contemporary can create a beautiful look all on its own.

- **Freshen Up:** When searching for the perfect frames to group together, don't forget to scout sales racks at home design stores for interesting shapes. Or even try shopping the rooms of your own home for a new spin on a forgotten piece. You can bring new life to old frames by unifying them with varying shades of the same color. This applies to the matte in a frame, too. Don't let a blah color hold you back. Give it a spritz with spray paint; add stripes with painter's tape; or use a stencil for a bold, unexpected statement.

2. Numbers

- **Odd Numbers:** When dealing with groupings, odd numbers are known to play with the eye to create a more appealing display.

- **Even Numbers:** If you prefer symmetry on your walls, try even-numbered groupings. Always use pairings or equal numbers when going for a bold, simplistic statement, and a cleaner look.

- **Ratio:** When using frames together, remember this: One large frame paired with two smaller ones makes a great balanced look, even when working with odd numbers. Always consider this element in your groupings.

3. Display

- **Always at Eye Level:** The most common mistake we see is hanging art too high. Strive for eye level. When hanging frames in groups, always go for a spacing that keeps them closer, with the negative space greater on the outsides than in between.
- **Hanging over Furniture:** Keep frames and art no higher than 5 to 6 inches above a piece of furniture for a clean, intentional look.
- **Practice Makes Perfect:** Hanging things on the wall can sometimes feel laborious and downright intimidating. Don't be afraid to sketch it out for proportions, lay it on the floor, and measure. Cut pieces of paper to size and tape them to the wall to try it out. Ask your friends for another opinion. Small holes in walls are pretty forgiving in the grand scheme of things, so even if you mess up, there's a fix for that.

Above all, be brave, stay flexible, and just go for it. This is how we grow, learn, and create personal displays of beautiful, one-of-a-kind art in our homes!

It is our hope that, within the pages of this book, you find inspiration. If you're looking for your voice or maybe even a springboard to cultivate your home into a reflection of who you really are, we hope that you find something you're crazy about, let go of your fears, and love the home you create. And if you're looking for more design options or need help arranging these beautiful images, take a look at *Handmade Walls*, *The Custom Art Collection: Art for the Traditional Home*, and *The Custom Art Collection: Art for the Contemporary Home*, the companions to this title.

The walls of your home hold the potential for great beauty and we hope you feel passionate about the possibilities for beauty that lie within. After all, when you add something that speaks to you, it truly can take your space to an entirely different level of amazing. Art is the perfect place to begin . . . the ultimate inspiration.

Ashley *and* Jamin Mills

The Handmade Home:
Creating a Haven for the Every Day

Annie Bailey
"Auto Repair"

Tim McConnachie
"Rhino"

Tim McConnachie
"Giraffe"

Tim McConnachie
"Elephant"

Courtney Oquist
"Tribal Feather"

Sonja Caldwell
"Pink Rollercoaster"

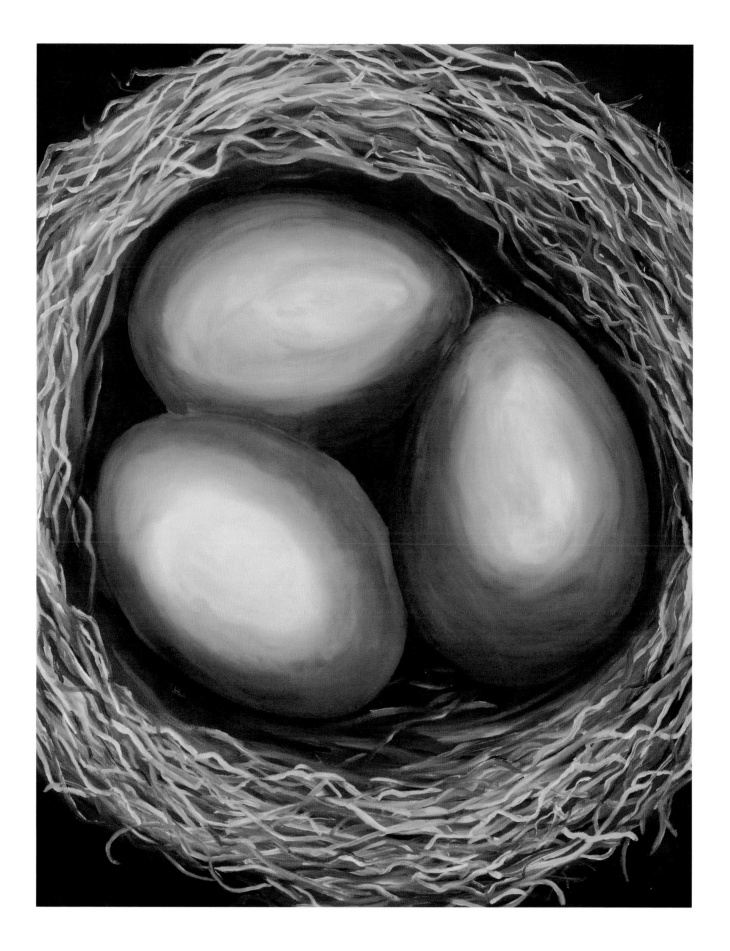

Ashley Mills
"Nest Eggs"

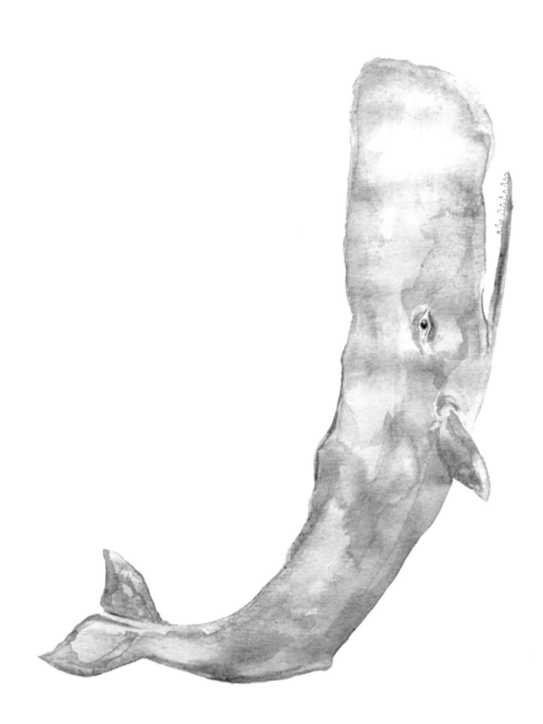

Sarah B. Martinez
"Sperm Whale"

Today you are You,
that is truer than true.
There is no one alive
who is youer than You.
—Dr. Seuss—

Joni Lay
"Flamingo Print"

Jennifer Lee
"Flower Power"

Emily Jones
"Dwell"

Emily Jones
"Birch Tree"

EXPAND
YOUR
VIEW

Jan Skácelík

Jan Skácelík
"Viewmaster"

····· YOU ARE ·····
BEAUTIFUL
INSIDE & OUT

Jan Skácelík

Jan Skácelík
"Mat Pink"

LIFE

IS

A *mixtape*

Jan Skácelík

Jan Škácelík
"Mixtape"

Amy Tyler
"Little"

Debbra Obertanec
"Red Door"

Jennifer Lee
"Star Jar"

Jennifer Lee
"All You Need"

Marianne LoMonaco
"Le Papillon"

Ashley Percival
"Owl Hipster"

Ashley Percival
"Bear and Pug"

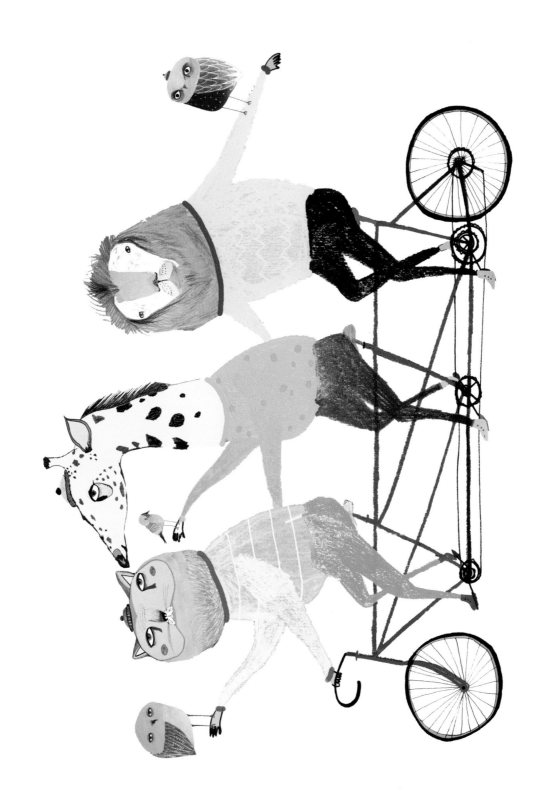

Annie Bailey
"Bikers"

Ashley Percival
"On the Line"

Ashley Mills
"Record Player"

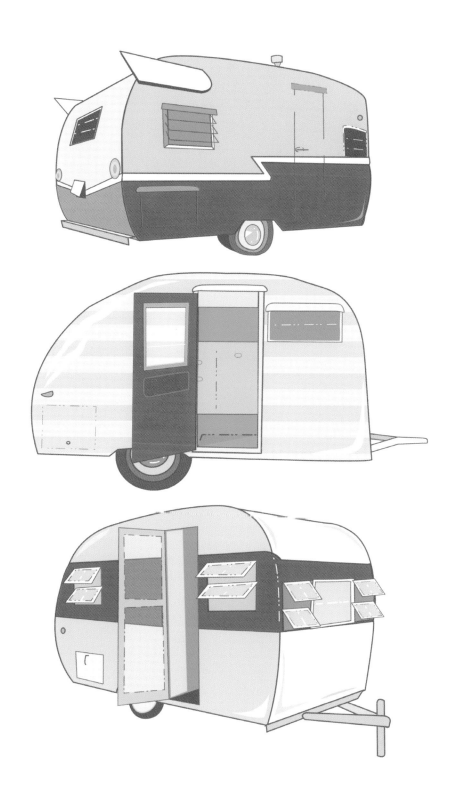

Ashley Mills
"Campers"

Ashley Mills
"Cameras"

Ashley Mills
"Cars"

Marianne LoMonaco
"The Camera Collector"

Courtney Oquist
"Green Owl"

Rachel Parker
"Roman Reverie"

Christine Lindstrom
"Be Here Now"

Michelle Tavares
"Seadragons"

Michelle Tavares
"Ampersand"

Michelle Tavares
"Octo Blue"

P. Cotterill

Patricia Cotterill
"Phone"

OH, IT'S A HAPPY DAY!

Stephanie Sliwinski
"Oh Happy Day"

Yellena James
"Brolly"

Yellena James
"Morning"

Sonja Caldwell
"Japanese Parasol"

Credits

Annie Bailey, *Montana Photo Journal*
"Auto Repair"
"On the Line"
www.mtphotojournal.etsy.com
Annie Bailey is the photographer for *Montana Photo Journal*. Her work is a reflection of a life spent surrounded by open space and blue sky. She was born and raised in Montana, with most of her life spent on her family's ranch in the Smith River valley. Seeing and documenting the tiny moments in life is what she wants to do for the rest of her life.

Sonja Caldwell
"Pink Rollercoaster"
"Japanese Parasol"
www.etsy.com/shop/sonjacaldwell
Sonja was born in Kansas but moved to Japan at age 7, then to California at age 10. She holds a BA in studio art from UC Davis. Being the daughter of a wanderlust and an international businessman, she has always enjoyed travel photography and has had a lot of opportunities to do it. As a photographer, her main subject is Paris, France. She splits her time between Paris and her home in San Jose, California.

Patricia Cotterill
"Phone"
PCotterill.Etsy.com
Born in Scotland, Patricia Cotterill lived in Europe, the Middle East and Asia before settling in Asheville, NC. This has left a deep impression on her painting approach. Light, shape, and color add to her canvas images of a moment captured in time; a diary of everyday life.

Yellena James
"Brolly"
"Morning"
www.Yellena.com
Yellena James grew up and attended art school in Sarajevo before moving to Portland, Oregon. Each intimate world she creates seems to posses its own ethos and its own special ability to radiate emotion. Her work explores intricate and delicate forms of an imaginary ecosystem, creating an ethereal place that is hauntingly familiar and yet hypnotically exotic. She's

done illustrations for many high-profile companies and has done gallery shows around the globe.

Joni Lay
"Flamingo Print"
www.LayBabyLay.com
Joni Lay is a designer and blogger focusing on inspired design for nurseries and children's rooms. She lives in Atlanta with her two daughters and husband, and enjoys encouraging others to add delight and imagination into their homes.

Jennifer Lee
"Flower Power"
"Star Jar"
"All You Need"
www.Jenndalyn.com
Jennifer Lee, creator of *Jenndalyn Art*, is a mixed media artist living and working in Columbus, Ohio. Inspired by nature, small miracles, and a general appreciation for all worldly things, her vibrant and colorful work aims to remind people to pay attention and notice the beauty that surrounds them every single day.

Emily Jones, *Jones Design Company*
"Dwell"
"Birch Tree"
www.JonesDesignCompany.com
Emily's love of childhood art grew into a small stationery business, which turned into a lifestyle blog. She creates original art prints, DIY projects, and delights in talking about home decorating, motherhood, blogging, and great design. Come for a visit at *www.jonesdesigncompany.com*, and hopefully you will leave encouraged and inspired.

Christine Lindstrom
"Be Here Now"
Shop.maiautumn.com
In 2009, Christine Lindstrom started her company, Mai Autumn, with the idea of making life a little more beautiful. She believes in savoring the small pleasures in life, lingering, exploring, and being surrounded by inspiring things. She was raised at the Jersey Shore and enjoys cooking, gardening, and reading many,

many books, all of which inspire her art greatly. She received her BA in painting in 2008 and is currently living in Ocean Grove, NJ.

Marianne LoMonaco
"The Camera Collector"
"Le Papillon"
www.MarianneLoMonaco.etsy.com
Marianne LoMonaco is a Toronto-born photographer. She is completely self-taught and in 2009, she finally upgraded her camera to one that actually worked. And fell in love. Hard and fast. Passionately in love. With photography. Completely driven to improve both creatively and technically, never satisfied for long without challenging herself. "It was that year I found a part of my life I was always meant to live."

Sarah B. Martinez
"Sperm Whale"
SarahBMartinez.com
After saying "goodbye" to city life and moving to the country in 2011, Sarah Martinez has brought her daydreams ot becoming a flourishing artist to life. She, her musician husband, and their tiny baby moved into a magical stone house in the Northwest hills of Connecticut, where she now muses from her sunny home studio. Along with earth and sky, the flora and fauna in between are her sweetest inspirations.

Tim McConnachie
"Rhino"
"Giraffe"
"Elephant"
www.AnimalCrewShop.com
Tim McConnachie grew up on a farm in Australia. From an early age he was drawing and won several awards during his childhood. He made his solo exhibition debut in Minneapolis when he was 21, with subsequent shows in New York City and Munich. He recently began a new series called "Animal Crew" that revisits his young love of animals.

Ashley Mills
"Nest Eggs"
"Record Player"
"Campers"
"Cameras"
"Cars"
www.thehandmadehome.net
Ashley mixes her love of art, great design, and writing into full-time fun at Thehandmade home.net. Here you'll find stories on a little bit of everything from the fun of parenthood to a love for everyday life.

Debbra Obertanec
"Red Door"
www.ShadeTreePhotography.Etsy.com
Debbra is a natural light photographer who finds inspiration everywhere, from soft colors and light, nature and the changing seasons, to some of the simplest images of vintage days gone by. It is easier for her to capture life with the camera than to put it into words. She is happiest and most creative behind the lens. Life is truly fleeting; capturing these images has allowed her to remember the tiny, intricate details that may have been lost or forgotten in the moment.

Courtney Oquist
"Tribal Feather"
"Green Owl"
"Birch Trees"
www.CourtneyOquist.Etsy.com
Courtney Oquist is an artist and art teacher based in Huntington Beach, CA. Through painting and drawing, Courtney explores the fantastical and eccentric part of everyday ness. She is inspired by nature, by people, by beauty, and especially by color and the meditative act of painting.

Rachel Parker
"Roman Reverie"
www.RachelsStudio.com
Rachel Parker is a self-taught artist who works mainly in watercolors. As the daughter of an artist, she was raised going to painting lessons and watching her mother create. Her moti-vation for creation is to capture what may otherwise go unnoticed; to reveal the beauty in simple moments and objects. Making an image come alive on paper is her inspiration. Rachel has sold her work nationally and inter-nationally through www.rachelsstudio.com.

Ashley Percival
"Owl Hipster"
"Bear and Pug"
"Bikers"
www.etsy.com/uk/shop/
AshleyPercival?ref=si_shop
Ashley Percival is a freelance illustrator from England. His artwork is suitable for all ages and has been described as fun, unique, and quirky. He has had his art licensed for a range of products including home decor, wall art, clothing, stationery, and watches.

Jan Skácelík
"Viewmaster"
"Mat Pink"
"Mixtape"
www.etsy.com/shop/handz
Jan Skácelík is a graphic designer from Olo-mouc, a small city in the Czech Republic. After studying graphic design, she worked in many graphic studios until finally her passion for Scandinavian design, mid century mod-ern, and pop culture design brought her to making her retro-inspired art prints.

Stephanie Sliwinski, *Fancy That Design House & Co.*
"Oh Happy Day"
www.FancyThatDesignHouse.Etsy.com
Stephanie Sliwinski is owner/designer of Fancy That Design House & Co., near Mil-waukee, WI. Her childhood love of drawing rainbows and unicorns led her to a degree in both art and graphic communication. Upon graduation, she worked full time, cre-ating apparel graphics for a wide variety of national retail accounts. These days, she is wife to an amazingly supportive husband, Chad, and mother of two young boys, Colton & Beckham. When she is not playing superheroes or stepping on Legos, she can be found designing graphics full of elements she loves—color, texture, typography, and personal meaning.

Michelle Tavares
"Seadragons"
"Ampersand"
"Octo Blue"
www.etsy.com/shop/calamaristudio
Michelle Tavares, the artist behind Calamari Studio, grew up in southern California and studied illustration and design at Utah Val-ley University. She now enjoys a somewhat nomadic life with her husband, Spencer, and their two sons. Michelle is most inspired by the intricacy of nature and more of her work can be seen at Etsy.com/calamaristudio.

Amy Tyler, *Amy Tyler Photography*
"Little"
www.AmyTylerPhotography.Etsy.com
As a young adult, Amy studied fine art at Middle Tennessee State University. After spending many years as an oil pastel artist, she transitioned into photography. It was there, behind the lens of her first camera, where she truly fell in love. Amy's favorite part of photography is the post-production editing work on her computer, where her fine art background really comes into play. She loves photographing all things delicate and sweet, which led her to specialize in nursery decor.

Acknowledgments

To the amazingly talented artists who were gracious enough to share their beautiful creations with all of us: thank you. This book would not be possible without you.

To the wonderful team at Adams Media for their insight, patience, and seeing something in us, we are so humbled. You have been a delight.

And to our inspiring readers, we are forever awed and grateful for all of you.

Thank you.

About the Authors

Jamin and Ashley Mills began their adventure together as college sweethearts. After a decade of marriage and three offspring later, they currently reside with their family in Montgomery, Alabama. They are the voices behind this book and their website, *www.thehandmadehome.net.*

At The Handmade Home, they share their daily journey and down-to-earth passion as the parents to three incredible children and one crazy dog. In between the mountainous piles of dirty laundry and musical bed fiascos with their glorious little troublemakers, they're also known for their handmade revamps and one-of-a-kind projects as they create a haven for the everyday.

For more inspiring projects and one-of-a-kind creations, visit The Handmade Home at *www.thehandmadehome.net.*

Ashley *and* **Jamin Mills**
The Handmade Home:
Creating a Haven for the Every Day

Bid farewell to blank walls and say hello to the art you love—all at an exceptional value.

The Custom Art Collection makes it easy and inexpensive for you to find the perfect print for every corner of your home. Featuring curated collections for contemporary, eclectic, and traditional homes, each book in this lovely series showcases original artwork from up-and-coming artists and pairs the prints with others in the collection to complete the look.

Art for the Contemporary Home
Trade Paperback
978-1-4405-7090-6, $22.99

Art for the Traditional Home
Trade Paperback
978-1-4405-7088-9, $22.99

Beautiful DIY Décor for a One-of-a-Kind Home

Perfect for those who want to fill their space with unique personality, *Handmade Walls* offers 22 fabulous DIY projects—each easy enough to achieve in a day. Get that creative look you've always wanted without spending a fortune or succumbing to cookie-cutter designs. Your dream home design is within reach!

Handmade Walls
Trade Paperback
978-1-4405-7232-6, $24.99